LIFE SCIENCE

The Rescue of Dindim the Penguin

MICHÈLE DUFRESNE

TABLE OF CONTENTS

Caught in an Oil Spill 2
Mr. João 4
Released 8
Gone and Back Again 14
Victims of Pollution 18
Glossary/Index 20

PIONEER VALLEY EDUCATIONAL PRESS, INC

CAUGHT IN AN OIL SPILL

In May 2011, a small penguin was swimming in the ocean when he was caught in an oil spill.

These penguins are covered in oil from an oil spill. Once their feathers are covered with oil, it will be very difficult for them to swim.

The oil covered his feathers and made it impossible for him to swim. He washed up on a beach on the coast of **Brazil**.

MORE TO EXPLORE

Here is an **OIL PLATFORM**. From the platform, workers drill for oil at the bottom of the ocean.

MR. JOÃO

One very hot and sunny day,
a man named Mr. João
found the penguin on the beach.
There were vultures nearby, looking for dead
animals to eat. The penguin looked dead.

But when he looked closer,
Mr. João realized that the penguin
was still alive! He moved the penguin
to the shade, away from the vultures.

After a few hours, the penguin
had not recovered.

Image owned by Globo

Dindim was a Magellanic penguin. Magellanic penguins were named after the **EXPLORER** Ferdinand Magellan, who spotted the birds in 1520 when he was exploring South America.

MORE TO EXPLORE

Mr. João was a kind and gentle man. He could not leave the young penguin there to die. Mr. João took the penguin back to his house.

Mr. João washed the oil off the penguin's feathers and fed him sardines. Over the next few days, the penguin grew stronger.

More to Explore

Adult Magellanic penguins have black backs and white **ABDOMENS**. They have a black horseshoe-shaped band on their front and a thick black band under their chin.

Image owned by Globo

Mr. João had a two-year-old grandson who could not say "pinguim" (*PEEN-gweem*), the **Portuguese** word for penguin. He called the penguin "Dindim."

RELEASED

After a few days, Dindim seemed strong enough to live on his own. Mr. João took Dindim to a nearby island and released him into the sea.

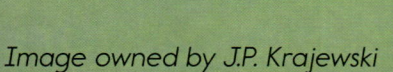
Image owned by J.P. Krajewski

Later that day, after returning home, Mr. João heard squeaking in his backyard. Dindim had returned and was calling out for him!

Image owned by Globo

MORE TO EXPLORE

Magellanic penguins are known for their loud, **MOURNFUL** calls. They sometimes sound like a donkey.

Dindim stayed in Mr. João's backyard.
He played on the beach
and swam in the water every day.

GONE AND BACK AGAIN

One day in March, Dindim disappeared.
No one knew where he had gone.
Everyone thought he had left for good.

But a few months later, Mr. João heard a loud squeak in his backyard. Dindim had returned!

Mr. João was very happy to see his special friend again.

Image owned by J.P. Krajewski

Image owned by J.P. Krajewski

Every year, Dindim returns to Mr. João in late June and stays with him until March.

But why does he return? A scientist who studies wildlife has met Mr. João and Dindim. He has an explanation for why Dindim comes back every year.

According to the scientist, Magellanic penguins are usually very loyal to their partner.

Professor J.P. Krajewski photographing penguins

They live for more than 25 years, and usually the same couple nests in the same hole every summer.

Instead of going to his usual nesting site, Dindim returns to the place where he was rescued and fed in Brazil. His rescuer, Mr. João, is now like family to him.

VICTIMS OF POLLUTION

Unfortunately, Dindim is just one of the thousands of **marine** animals that have been victims of pollution. Oil spills kill more than 40,000 penguins every year.

Many animals get sick from eating plastic.
They can get trapped in fishing nets
or covered in oil from oil spills in the ocean.
They all need our attention and help.
They need us to rescue them
like Mr. João rescued Dindim.

1 Most Magellanic penguins mate for life.

4 Once the chicks hatch, they begin to grow feathers.

6 After about 40 to 70 days, the penguins head out to sea.

MAGELLANIC PENGUINS

2 After mating, two eggs are usually laid.

3 The male and female take turns caring for the eggs while the other hunts for food.

5 Once the chicks have some feathers, the parents leave them and return to feed them every one to three days.

GLOSSARY

abdomens
areas where the stomach is located in the body

Brazil
a country in South America

explorer
someone who travels to a place to learn about it

marine
plants or animals that live in the sea

mournful
sad

Portuguese
a language spoken by people in Brazil and other countries

INDEX

abdomens 6
beach 3, 4, 12
Brazil 3, 17
coast 3
explorer 5
feathers 2, 3, 6
marine 18

Magellanic penguin 2, 5, 6, 11, 16
mournful 11
nests 17
Professor Krajewski 16
Portuguese 7
ocean 2, 3, 19

oil spill 2, 18-19
sardines 6
vultures 4